A Robbie Reader

Meet Our New Student From

MEXICO

Tamra Orr

P.O. Box 196
Hockessin, Delaware 19707
Visit us on the web: www.mitchelllane.com
Comments? email us: mitchelllane@mitchelllane.com

Meet Our New Student From

Australia • China • Colombia • Great Britain • Haiti • Israel • Korea • Malaysia • **Mexico** • New Zealand • Nigeria • Tanzania

PUBLISHER'S NOTE: The facts on which the story in this book is based have been thoroughly researched. Documentation of such research can be found on page 44. While every possible effort has been made to ensure accuracy, the publisher will not assume liability for damages caused by inaccuracies in the data, and makes no warranty on the accuracy of the information contained herein.

To reflect current usage, we have chosen to use the secular era designations BCE ("before the common era") and CE ("of the common era") instead of the traditional designations BC ("before Christ") and AD (*anno Domini*, "in the year of the Lord").

Library of Congress Cataloging-in-Publication Data

Orr, Tamra.
  Meet our new student from Mexico / by Tamra Orr.
    p. cm. —(A Robbie reader)
  Includes bibliographical references and index.
  ISBN 978-1-58415-646-8 (library bound)
  1. Mexico—Juvenile literature. I. Title.
  F1208.5.O77 2008
  972—dc22
                                    2008002820

Printing   1   2   3   4   5   6   7   8   9

PLB

CONTENTS

Mexico

Mexico is a lively, festive land. The people celebrate holidays such as Cinco de Mayo with traditional dancing and spicy, colorful food.

Keeping a
Secret

Chapter 1

Kimberly smiled. She had done it! She had kept her secret for two whole months. There were times when she thought she would not be able to stay quiet another hour, but she had. Mrs. Turner had told her that since she had done such a good job, she could tell the class the big news.

"Good morning, Kimberly," said Mrs. Turner as Kim walked into the room. She gave her a special smile. It made Kim feel very important.

After attendance was taken, Mrs. Turner got the class's attention. "You all know we have a new student coming next week," she said. "She is coming from a place called the Yucatán. It is in Mexico. I think I will let Kimberly tell you about her though, because she knows her the best."

Kim got up and walked to the front of the room. She knew everyone was looking at her and wondering how she knew something that they did not. "The girl

Mexico City is one of the busiest cities in the entire world. Long ago it was the Aztec capital, Tenochtitlán.

The violin plays an important role in the mariachi band, which performs a type of music that is very popular in Mexico. The band may also have trumpets, a Mexican guitar, a *vihuela* (a high-pitched, five-string guitar), and a *guitarrón* (a small-scaled bass guitar). These bands usually play lively traditional Mexican folk songs or love songs.

who is coming is named Marisa Tómas. I have never met her, but she is one of my best friends."

"That doesn't make sense," said Linda.

"How can you be friends with someone you've never met?" asked Rosalie.

Kim knew they would ask her that. She held up some envelopes. "This is how," she said. "We've been pen pals for the last two years. We write letters to each other. We've sent each other pictures of our pets.

According to the legend, this Montezuma cypress was called the Tule tree. Tule stands for Tú Uniras Los Enemigos, or "You will unite the enemies." The 2,000-year-old tree grows on the church grounds of Santa Maria del Tule in the state of Oaxaca.

We've exchanged postcards. I always send her a card for her birthday, and she sends me one for mine. It's been a lot of fun."

"Why is she coming to our school? Is she coming just to visit you?" asked Judea.

"Her family is moving here," replied Kim. "Her dad has a job here already, and now Marisa and her mom are joining him. I can't wait!"

"We're all excited," said Mrs. Turner. "I think we need to show Marisa how happy we are to have her when she arrives, too. Can anyone think of a way to do that?"

"I think we should make a big Welcome sign and put it up on the front doors of the school," suggested Cory.

"Let's make a special Mexican treat for her to eat at snack time," said Katherine.

"Hey! I know," said Peter. "Let's make her a **piñata**. I had one for my birthday party, and my dad told me they are a Mexican tradition."

"Those are all great ideas," said Mrs. Turner. "Let's write them down on the blackboard and see what we have to do to get them done."

Kim smiled. She could hardly wait to see her friend. Now her whole class was counting the hours before her arrival, just as Kim was.

A fifteenth-century gold pendant made to honor the Aztec god of the dead, Mictlantecuhtli. It is one of the very few gold ornaments that was not melted down by the Spanish conquistadores.

A Struggle for Independence

Chapter 2

The first people to live in the area we know now as Mexico arrived before 8000 BCE. They were Olmecs and Teotihuacáns (tay-oh-tee-wah-KAHNS), who came north from South America. They were following herds of buffalo and other large animals, which they hunted for food. Over the next thousand years, the weather got hotter. Rain did not fall as often. The dry ground could not grow enough grass to feed all the large animals. The animals began to disappear, so the tribes, which now included Mayans and Aztecs, began to hunt less and farm more. They planted corn, beans, peppers, and tomatoes.

As time went by, villages grew. People began to make pottery. Some wove baskets. They also built **temples** in which to worship their gods of rain and sun. Some of the groups also built huge **pyramids**. There was a great deal of fighting over who ruled what lands. **Empires** rose and fell.

In 1517, Diego Velázquez, an adventurer from Spain, was living on the island of Cuba. He had heard there were treasures to be found in a land to the west. He sent an expedition (ek-speh-DIH-shun) to Mexico to search for those treasures. When the explorers brought back Aztec gold, Velázquez sent Hernando Cortés with 300 men to find more. The Spaniards brought guns and horses and ferocious dogs called mastiffs—

The ancient Maya were intelligent and creative. They invented accurate calendars (pictured). The Spanish conquerors destroyed the majority of these valuable pieces of Mayan art and culture.

In 1519, Spanish conquistador Hernando Cortés (left) met with the last Aztec emperor, Montezuma II.

things the native peoples had never seen before. It did not take long for the Spaniards to conquer the Aztec leader, Montezuma, and his people. The surviving Aztecs became slaves to the Spaniards.

Population Changes

For the next 300 years, Mexico's territories remained under the control of Spain. By 1650, the native population had dwindled, due to fighting and disease. At the same time, the Spanish population kept growing. Finally, in 1810, urged by a priest named Miguel Hildalgo y Castilla, the peasants and original people of Mexico decided they had had enough. They wanted to rule their lands again. Just before dawn on September 16, Castilla had all of the Spaniards in the village of Dolores arrested. Then he rang the church bell to tell the Mexican Indians that it was time to rise up and get revenge. Today, more than a century later, September 16 is remembered in Mexico as Independence Day.

The revolt did not work. The Spanish king stayed on the throne. It was not until 1821 that Mexico was finally allowed to be independent. In 1824, Mexicans elected their own president.

Finding Independence

During the early 1800s, Spain controlled not only Mexico, but also Texas, New Mexico, and California.

A great deal of the population included people from various parts of the United States. When Antonio López de Santa Anna, the Mexican leader, decided to change the constitution so that he would have more control over the land, these Americans did not like it. Although he was able to beat the American rebels at the battle of the Alamo, it was a short victory. Santa Anna was defeated later that year at San Jacinto. Finally, Texas was independent from Mexico. Relationships between Mexico and the

In March 1847, during the Mexican-American War, General Winfield Scott led a twenty-day siege into the Mexican seaport of Vera Cruz. The city surrendered, and soon the U.S. troops marched inland to Mexico City.

While Benito Juárez was president of Mexico, the French tried to march into Mexico City and turn the country into a French colony. At the Battle of Puebla, the Mexican soldiers forced the French to retreat. That day, May 5, 1862, is celebrated in Mexico as Cinco de Mayo (the Fifth of May).

United States began to sour. In 1846, the U.S. declared war on Mexico. When it ended two years later, Mexico had lost a lot of its land in the north to the United States.

What was left of Mexico was governed by Benito Juárez, who was elected president in 1861. He pushed for many changes, including taking back some of the churches from the Roman Catholics. His leadership was followed by a mix of people, from Austrian Archduke Maximillian to **dictator** Porfirio Díaz. In the 1900s, a series of presidents worked to make Mexico's **economy** (ee-KAH-nuh-mee) stronger.

By the time World War II began in 1939, Mexico was doing well. It built new factories. It made war equipment. After the war, the country kept developing. New buildings went up, and roads, highways, and railroad tracks were constructed. In the 1970s, oil was found, which helped to bring more money and jobs into Mexico.

Sure that its financial future was secure, the country borrowed a lot of money. However, the oil that was found turned out to be of low grade, and by the mid-1980s, Mexico was in big trouble. A huge earthquake in 1985 did not help matters. It caused billions of dollars' worth of damage and the people were not happy with the government's response to the quake. Twenty years later, Mexico was still struggling to find enough resources for all of its people.

Mexican Independence Day begins every September 15 at 11:00 P.M. all across Mexico, celebrating El Grito— Father Hidalgo's cry for independence, "Mexicanos, Viva Mexico!" (Mexicans, long live Mexico!). The president rings the same bell that Father Hidalgo rang to call the people in 1810. The celebration lasts through the next day, with parades, bullfights, and fireworks.

A Large and
Lovely Land

Chapter

3

Mexico is southwest of the United States. It touches the borders of California, Arizona, and Texas. Winding like a ribbon to separate the two countries is a river called the Rio Grande. South of Mexico are the Central American countries of Belize and Guatemala. Mexico is more than three times the size of Texas and is home to more than 100 million people.

The biggest city in Mexico is the country's capital, Mexico City. It is very crowded, with 8.7 million people living there. It is 7,342 feet above sea level—as high as some mountains. When people come to visit, they notice that the air is thinner, so it is a little harder to breathe. They have to get used to the change.

Mexico City is busy, with buses, taxis, and people jamming the streets. The city holds a mixture of ancient and modern architecture. Right next to a tall skyscraper, you might see an Aztec stone figure or a Spanish-style palace.

**United States
of America**

Tijuana
California
Arizona
Mexicali

Texas

Rio Grande

Baja
California

Chihuahua

Laredo

Rio Grande

*Gulf of
Mexico*

La Paz
Cabo San Lucas

Mexico

Guadalajara

Mérida • Cancún
Uxmal • Cozumel
Chichén Itzá

PACIFIC OCEAN

Mexico City ✪

Oaxaca
Acapulco

Belize

Guatemala

Where in the World

Yucatán Peninsula

FACTS ABOUT MEXICO

Official Name: United Mexican States
(Estados Unidos Mexicanos)

Total Area: 761,600 square miles
(1,972,550 square kilometers)

Population: 108,700,891 (July 2007 est.)

Capital: Mexico City

Religions: Roman Catholicism,
Protestantism

Languages: Spanish; various Mayan,
Nahuatl, and other regional languages

Chief Exports: Manufactured goods, oil
and oil products, silver, fruits, vegetables,
coffee, cotton

Monetary Unit: Mexican peso

In the eastern part of Mexico is the Yucatán **Peninsula**. There, Mayan stone temples still stand. Legend says the Pyramid of the Magician, in Uxmal, was built by a magical dwarf. The main city in the Yucatán, Mérida, is known for its unusual plants and trees. For example, the **chicle** tree grows there. The liquid inside it was used to make chewing gum. The sisal plant grows there also. Its fibers are stripped and twisted to make ropes, bags, and hats.

The name *chicle* comes from a Nahuatl word for "gum" or "sticky stuff." It was a well known plant to the Aztecs and Mayans. Even the early European settlers recognized it for its flavor and high sugar content. For many years, it was used by a number of companies to make chewing gum.

Chapter 3

The Mayans built a pyramid honoring their serpent-god Kukulkan in Chichén Itzá. In the afternoon of the spring and fall equinoxes, an amazing thing happens at this pyramid. The sunlight hits the western side of the main staircase. The shadow creates seven triangles that look like the body of a serpent 37 yards long. As the light moves, the snake appears to creep down the stairs until it joins the head carved in the stone at the bottom.

East of Mérida is Chichén Itzá. It has a sacred well in which treasures were thrown as sacrifices to the Mayan gods. There is an ancient Toltec ball court where vicious ball games were played. Along the coastline, Cancún has become a popular vacation spot. Once it was a home for pirates, but now it is known for scuba diving.

In the western part of Mexico is the country's second largest city, Guadalajara. Mariachi (mayr-ee-AH-chee) bands stroll along on the city streets, singing and playing trumpets, guitars, and violins. There are farms in this area too, and the cowboys are called *charros* (CHAR-ohs). Some of them show off their riding and roping skills at the *charreada* (char-ee-AY-dah), or rodeo.

In the northwestern part of Mexico, there is a long strip of land called Baja California.

It is so hot in the east that many people sleep outside their houses in hammocks. Hammocks are sold by street vendors.

Almost 3 million people live on this peninsula, most of them in Tijuana or Mexicali. There are beautiful mountains on Baja California. The tallest one is the Devil's Peak, which soars more than 10,000 feet up into the sky. This is a land of wet and dry. Surrounded by water on three sides, it still has four deserts that span it. Millions of years ago, the land was attached to Mexico. As the earth's plates have moved, the landmass has been pushed 300 miles from where it started.

The world's second largest coral reef is near Cancún. It is home to limestone caverns, deep tunnels, and unusual black coral.

Mexico

Mexican food is a delicious combination of bread-like tortillas, fresh guacamole, and a salsa known as pico de gallo. These ingredients, along with beans and rice, make up a variety of dishes, such as burritos, tacos, and fajitas.

A Close-up
Look

Chapter

Life in Mexico is a lively mix of many things. People there eat fresh, spicy food. Many grow their own food on farms. They enjoy year-round warm weather. In Mexico, people can hear different languages, visit villages full of **adobe** (uh-DOH-bee) houses, and of course—just like in the United States—go to school.

Nachos, Anyone?

Mexican foods are actually quite familiar to many Americans. Mexican restaurants have popped up all over the United States, serving **burritos** covered in **picante** sauce, crunchy tacos with **salsa**, and plates of **nachos** with sour cream on top.

Thousands of years ago, the Mexicans learned to rely on corn, and they still do. **Tortillas** are made from corn, and they are eaten plain, fried for a taco, warmed to make a burrito, or deep-fried to make a **tostada**. **Frijoles** (free-HOH-leez), or beans, are also common. They are boiled, mashed, fried, and then sometimes refried. The people of Mexico also eat atole (aa-TOH-lay), a thick cornmeal dish, and tamales (tuh-MAA-leez), cornmeal and meat steamed inside a corn husk. Other food favorites include avocados, bananas, and papayas. While coffee and soda are popular there, so are fruit juices and cinnamon-flavored hot chocolate.

Pico de gallo is a spicy vegetable topping that is added to many Mexican dishes to make them taste fresh and flavorful.

On October 21, 2005, Hurricane Wilma came ashore in Mexico. The wind and drenching rains—more than two feet of rain in some places—caused terrible damage on Cozumel and the Yucatán Peninsula.

Weather Zones

There are many different climates throughout Mexico. Much of the weather depends on the area's **elevation**, or how high above sea level it is. The higher one goes, the colder it gets. Up in the mountains, the temperatures are quite cold. The highest peaks are covered with snow year round.

Much of the country is very hot, with long summers and almost no winter at all. Rain falls in the summer in powerful, brief afternoon showers.

A colorfully dressed girl carries her younger brother or sister as she goes through town selling handmade baskets for money.

The coast and lowlands are the hottest areas, with temperatures ranging from the low 60s to over 100 degrees Fahrenheit. As the land rises, the temperatures drop. The temperate zone, or the area between 3,000 and 6,000 feet above sea level, is where most of the crops are planted. In places that are higher, like Mexico City, the temperatures are much cooler.

A Mix of Words
Most Mexicans speak Spanish, and many of them also speak English. However, because the land was first settled by a mix of peoples (such as the Aztecs, Maya, Olmec, and Teotihuacáns), there are other languages spoken here and there. More than five million people in Mexico speak a traditional tribal language. It may be Mayan, Nahuatl, or other types called Mixtec, Tarascan, and Zapotec.

Mexican Living
It is common for generations to live together in Mexico. Because there are so many people there and not enough houses, families often share the same home.

Homes in the city may be made out of adobe, or sun-dried clay. In the back may be a **patio** where the family spends a lot of time. Patios often have flowers, potted plants, and sometimes even a fountain. Some people in the largest cities are not this lucky, however.

The poorest people live in homes made out of scraps of wood and metal. It is not unusual for Mexican parents to work two or three jobs each to make enough money to support their families.

About one-fourth of Mexico's people live on a farm or in a small village. If you lived there, you would probably count the days until you could move into the city, where there is more to do and a better chance of getting a job. Many young people leave the farm early. Most villages are very simple, with dirt

This adobe community keeps people close together as their clay walls bake under the hot Mexican sun.

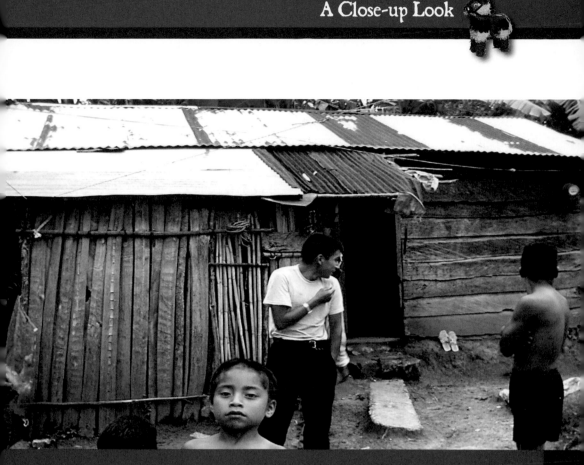

A number of Mexican families struggle to make enough money to keep their families fed. Their homes are fragile and made out of little more than wood and metal.

roads leading into and out of them. The marketplace is the center of life there, and families typically shop there once a week. They will trade food or clothes, or even handmade baskets or lace.

Village homes are very simple. They are made out of brick or cement blocks with straw or tile roofs. The floors are dirt, and windows are rare. Cooking fires are either built on the floor of the house or put outside, with poles holding large pots over them.

Time for School

School is important in Mexico, but the older the children get, the less they go. Most children go to elementary school, but fewer than half of them finish junior high. Very few graduate from high school or go on to college.

Mexico is a fascinating place where many Mexicans struggle to make a living, yet thousands of tourists come to visit each year. Many Mexicans come to the United States to look for a new start and a better life.

A classroom full of Mexican students show big smiles and eager faces—like classrooms of students all across the globe.

Fernando Valenzuela, L.A. Dodger

Fernando Valenzuela was known for his screwball—a special pitch that spins in the opposite direction of a curveball. He was born Fernando Valenzuela Anguamea in 1960 in the small village of Etchohuaquila in Sonora, Mexico. After playing for several Mexican teams, he joined the Los Angeles Dodgers in 1979. For a time he was so popular that baseball fans were crazy about getting his rookie baseball card. This craze was called Fernandomania. Nicknamed "El Toro" ("The Bull"), he became one of the league's best pitchers. In his later years, Valenzuela played for other teams and was on the coaching staff of Team Mexico. His son Fernando Jr. is a first baseman in Major League Baseball. He has played for the San Diego Padres and the St. Paul Saints.

Piñatas are a fun addition to any party. Filled with treats of all different kinds, they bring lots of laughs as kids try their best to break them open.

Bienvenido a neustra clase, *Marisa!*

Chapter 5

The banner was hung across the front of the school. It said: Welcome to Lewis and Clark Elementary School. Everyone in Kim's class had signed it. The snack was ready to be served. The piñata was hanging in the middle of the room. We had filled it with colorful erasers as prizes for later. A copy of the Mexican flag hung across the front blackboard, and a list of Spanish words was written on the one in back.

English	Spanish
Welcome to our class	*Bienvenido a nuestra clase* (b'-YEN-vay-nee-doh-ah-noo-ES-trah KLAH-say)
Hello	*Hola* (OH-lah)
My name is	*Mi nombre es* (mee NOM-bray es)
Good afternoon	*Buenas tardes* (b'WAY-nahs TAR-days)
Thank you	*Gracias* (GRAH-see-ahs)
Excuse me	*Perdoneme* (per-DOH-nay-may)

All the hard work and learning had been worth it. Marisa was thrilled to be in her new classroom, and her smile told everyone she truly felt welcome.

Ciclos de la vida

De huevo

Piloncillo is a special type of sugar that is pressed into cones and used to sweeten and flavor Mexican main dishes, desserts, and drinks. It adds a unique brown-sugar flavor.

I was waiting for Marisa at the front door of the school. We had had dinner together the night before, and even though she spoke English with an accent, I could understand most of what she said. Giggling was also no problem—we sounded just the same! I found out that she likes cheeseburgers, and she found out I love burritos. She is even more fun in person than in letters.

Marisa walked through the doors and, right away, I knew she was nervous. When she saw me standing there, though, she smiled. "*Hola, mi amiga,*" she said. I knew that meant, "Hello, my friend." I gave her a hug. While her mother went in to talk to the principal, I walked Marisa to our classroom. I opened the door and everyone stopped talking. Marisa stopped too. She squeezed my hand tightly. I squeezed back.

"Marisa, *bienvenido a nuestra clase!*" said Mrs. Turner. Marisa lit up. She smiled and walked into the classroom. She saw the plate of food on the table and her grin got even bigger. She glanced at the flag, then at the piñata hanging from the center of the room.

"*Son todos mis nuevos amigos,*" said Marisa. Some of the kids looked puzzled. Before I could figure out what she meant, Marisa slowly said, "You are all my new friends." Everyone started to smile. After all, friendship is a language that anyone can speak!

Flag of Mexico

How To Make

Chips & Guacamole
A Mexican Snack

Instructions

Most people who live in Mexico often eat foods that are made with beans, rice, and tortillas. They will also add salsa, a spicy dip made from peppers, onions, and tomatoes, plus **guacamole** (gwah-kuh-MOH-lee), a dip made from avocados. Here is a simple recipe for guacamole.

1. Have **an adult** cut the avocados and tomatoes into small pieces. Put them in a bowl. (Save the avocado pits.)
2. Have **an adult** cut the lime in half. Squeeze the juice into the bowl.
3. Add the sour cream, cumin, and salsa, then mash it all together.
4. Now grab some chips and start dipping!

If you have leftover guacamole, place the avocado pits on the dip and cover the bowl. Store the dip in the refrigerator. The pits will keep the guacamole from turning brown.

Things You Will Need

An adult to help you

Knife

Cutting board

Bowl

Spoon

Ingredients

2 avocados

2 tomatoes

1 lime

1 tablespoon sour cream

pinch of cumin (a spice)

1 tablespoon salsa

tortilla chips

Make Your Own
Piñata

You Will Need

Large Balloons

String

Yarn

Newspaper Strips

Flour

3 Cups of Water

Craft Paint and Brush

Stickers

There are a number of stories about how piñatas were invented. The tradition may have come to Mexico from Spain, but there was also an Aztec tradition using clay pots. A pot covered with feathers and filled with little treasures was raised on a pole to honor the Aztec war god Huitzilopochtli. When the pot was broken, the treats inside would fall to the feet of a statue of the god as an offering.

Instructions for Making a Piñata

 Blow up the balloon and tie it at the neck. Tie a string to the balloon.

 Make a thick paste with the flour and water.

 Dip the newspaper strips into the paste. Use the strips to cover the whole balloon except for a hole near the string. Apply one layer at a time, and let each layer dry for 24 hours. Make two layers like this.

 When the second layer is dry, wrap the balloon with yarn to give it strength. Put on another two layers of newspaper. Let them dry another 24 hours.

 Pop and remove the balloon. Decorate the piñata with paint, sparkles, stickers, or whatever you want.

 Fill the piñata with candy or other small surprises. Now it is ready to hang up for your next party!

Further Reading

Books

Auch, Alison. *Welcome to Mexico*. Mankato, Minnesota: Compass Point Books, 2002.

Brooks, Susie. *Mexico*. London: Chrysalis Children's Books, 2005.

Brown, Sally. *Alexandra's Travel Adventure: Making Friends in Mexico*. Cincinnati, Ohio: Emmis Books, 2005.

Johnston, Tony. *My Mexico*. New York: Putnam Juvenile, 1999.

McAlister, Caroline. *Holy Mole! A Folktale from Mexico*. Atlanta, Georgia: August House, 2007.

Parker, Edward. *The Changing Face of Mexico*. London: Hodder Wayland, 2004.

Turck, Mary C. *Mexico and Central America: A Fiesta of Cultures, Crafts and Activities for Ages 8–12*. Chicago: Chicago Review Press, 2004.

Works Consulted

Coe, Michael. *Mexico: From the Olmecs to the Aztecs*. New York: Thames and Hudson, 2002.

Franz, Carl. *The People's Guide to Mexico*. Berkeley, California: Avalon Travel Publishing, 2006.

Let's Go, Inc. *Let's Go Mexico*. Cambridge, Massachusetts: Let's Go Publications, 2007.

Mexico Tourism Board: www.visitmexico.com

Noble, John, et al. *Lonely Planet Mexico*. Oakland, California: Lonely Planet Publications, 2006.

Orr, Tamra. *Great Hispanic-Americans*. Lincolnwood, Illinois: Publications International, 2005.
Lonely Planet Destination Guide

On the Internet

DeLange, George, and Audrey. *Tule Tree, Santa Maria del Tule, Oaxaca Mexico*
http://www.delange.org/Tule/Tule.htm

Lonely Planet Destination Guide
www.lonelyplanet.com/worldguide/destinations/north-america/mexico/

Mexico for Kids
www.elbalero.gob.mx/index_kids.html

Embassy

Embassy of Mexico
1911 Pennsylvania Ave NW
Washington, DC 20006
(202) 728-1600
http://portal.sre.gob.mx/usa/

Glossary

adobe (uh-DOH-bee)—Sun-dried clay usually used to make bricks for houses.

burrito (bur-EE-toh)—Meat and/or beans wrapped in a soft tortilla.

chicle (CHIH-kul) tree—A tree that has a substance in it used to make chewing gum.

conquistador (kahn-KEES-tuh-dor)—A Spanish conqueror, especially of Mexico. The plural is conquistadores (kahn-kees-tuh-DOR-eez).

dictator (DIK-tay-tor)—A person or ruler who holds absolute power in a government.

economy (ee-KAH-nuh-mee)—The flow of goods and money in an area.

elevation (el-uh-VAY-shun)—The height above sea level.

empire (EM-pyr)—A vast area of land and people ruled by one king, or emperor.

frijoles (free-HOH-leez)—Beans used in Mexican-style cooking.

nachos (NAH-chohs)—Corn chips, usually with various toppings.

patio (PAA-tee-oh)—Courtyard.

peninsula (peh-NIN-soo-luh)—A body of land with water on three sides.

picante (pih-KON-tee)—Sharp or spicy flavored, often used as a name for a Mexican sauce.

piñata (pin-YAH-tah)—A decorated container full of candy or other treats and made out of paper and cardboard that is purposefully broken during a game at parties.

salsa (SOL-suh)—A dip made with tomatoes, peppers, and onions.

temple (TEM-pul)—A place of worship.

tortilla (tor-TEE-yuh)—A flat corn or flour wrap.

tostada (toh-STAH-duh)—A deep-fried, crunchy tortilla.

Index

ABOUT THE AUTHOR

Tamra Orr is the author of more than 120 nonfiction books for children of all ages. She has a bachelor's degree in secondary education and English, and has written for all the top national testing companies in the United States. She lives in the Pacific Northwest with her kids and husband and spends as much time reading as she can. Being an author is the best possible job she can imagine. She has always been fascinated by the colorful country of Mexico.